CONCRETE ELEGANCE ONE

The **Concrete** Centre™

RIBA ☶ **Publishing**

A

FOREWORD

The Concrete Elegance lecture series is a Concrete Centre initiative in collaboration with The Building Centre Trust. The series has become a firm favourite with a regular audience of Architects and Engineers, eager to learn more about the ways in which concrete can be used to achieve elegant designs.

David Bennett, the series organiser and resident guru, has devised an excellent mix of projects which have formed the backbone of the talks by designers and specialists. Concrete has, for many, been discovered as a versatile material suited to a wide range of applications from small scale artefacts and sculptures, domestic scale architecture through to multi-storey buildings and landscapes where the current generation of concretes offers greater potential than ever.

Further Concrete Elegance lectures are planned to include European architectural projects, smaller domestic works and more art-based projects, revealing both passion and commitment to the imaginative use of concrete.

We are confident that the chosen topics featured here will inspire and renew interest in concrete's dynamic visual qualities.

See you at the next series.

Allan Haines
Head of Education, The Concrete Centre

c

ACKNOWLEDGEMENTS

The Concrete Centre wish to thank all the speakers for
their contribution to the success of the series, for supplying
the images and assisting with notes for the drafting of text.

For further information on future
Concrete Elegance programmes visit
www.concretecentre.com

Written and edited by
David Bennett,
David Bennett Associates

Booklet designed by
Kneath Associates

Thanks to Birkhauser – Publishers for Architecture, for granting
permission to use short edited summaries of text derived from
the book "The Art of Precast Concrete" (ISBN -10;7643-7150-1)
for the following three projects: Precast Concrete of The Scottish
Parliament Building, The Spiral Staircase, Copenhagen and The
Seonyu Footbridge, Seoul. All rights reserved

Published by
RIBA Publishing
15 Bonhill Street
London EC2P 4EA

ISBN 1 85946 196 4

Stock Code 57075

RIBA Publishing is a trading name of
RIBA Enterprises Ltd www.ribaenterprises.com

D

CONTENTS

CONCRETE ELEGANCE IS A SERIES OF ARCHITECTURAL PRESENTATIONS GIVEN AT THE BUILDING CENTRE BY LEADING DESIGNERS, INNOVATORS AND MANUFACTURERS OF CONCRETE.

E

OVERVIEW

Concrete as an architectural and structural material has gone through many changes and evolutions in its development over the years, but probably none more pronounced than in the past decade. There is renewed interest in concrete's plastic and aesthetic qualities in architecture today, helped and encouraged by the expressive way that two young architectural practices highlighted in this review have exploited its self-finished quality and form with great success. Both projects demonstrate that standard ready-mixed concrete and the right selection of formwork and placement techniques can produce award-winning architecture at affordable prices. What is also a revelation is that both architects have never designed or used exposed concrete before. What they did discover is that there is a wealth of knowledge within the concrete industry to tap into to give them the confidence and encouragement to realise their ambitions.

Concrete as a structural material has had to be redefined in recent years with the introduction into the world market of two new ultra high performance concretes – CRC and Ductal®. These products have set new performance standards and promoted new thinking on how such materials can be engineered and prefabricated to produce pencil-thin, lightweight structures that compare with structural steel. The case studies of the stunning Spiral Staircase in Copenhagen and taut concrete arch of the Seonyu Bridge in Seoul highlighted in this review, show the range and potential of these new concretes in building and civil engineering applications. We hope to see a structure exploiting these new concretes in the UK.

Art and sculpture reflect the changing patterns of social culture, scientific advancement and intellectual thinking through mankind's history, expressed as paintings on canvas, castings in bronze or toolings in marble. Photography, screen printing, video recording, industrial plastic, animal carcasses and hum-drum everyday objects in recent decades have replaced canvas and bronze to communicate modern art. Carole Vincent has been exploiting concrete colour, texture and geometric forms in sculpture for many years from her studio in Boscastle. Thanks to her many commissions and international reputation, concrete is fast becoming a material for artistic expression

3

appealing to potters, sculptors and painters alike. Alongside Carole Vincent's silky smooth, conical sculptures, the work of the young concrete artist David Undery's enamelled abstract paintings are highlighted to show just how expressive and sensuous etching, pigmenting and lacquering concrete can be. Such creativity can be an inspiration for façade panels on buildings, insitu kitchen worktops and casting concrete floors.

Art has been expressed in architecture over the centuries, often as figures carved in stone, stained glass in windows, statues placed on cornices, frescos painted on plaster and mosaics on the floor. Rarely has the structure or the shape of the external fabric of a modern building been consciously derived from artistic motivation. With the completion of the new Scottish Parliament Building in Edinburgh art has become the focus for the design of the precast boundary walls along Canongate and the west elevation of the MSP (Member of Scottish Parliament) Office Building. The making of the master moulds and of the liner for casting each bespoke panel was solved by using a special computer-guided routing tool

that came from the aerospace industry. Malling Products Ltd in partnership with Patterns and Moulds Ltd made the world's first bespoke precast panels requiring no labour or carpentry skills in mould making, drastically reducing the cost and time for forming bespoke precast concrete. The technology and the process by which this was achieved are highlighted in this review. The images of the Canongate Wall and the MSP Office boundary wall tell their own story.

In the presentation of future Concrete Elegance series we will be covering self-compacting concrete, glass reinforced concrete, innovative use of concrete on small projects and taking a look at the precast architecture in Northern Europe. For more details of these and other related events contact The Concrete Centre on www. concretecentre.com.

We hope that this booklet will renew your interest in concrete in all its many forms and expressions and inspire you with new challenges and possibilities.

David Bennett,

Scottish Parliament

© Scottish Parliamentary Corporate Body/Adam Elder

The Canongate Wall of The Scottish Parliament Building
David Shillito, Malling Products Ltd and Gary Lucas, Patterns and Moulds Ltd

The Scottish Parliament Building has been the most challenging and architecturally complex structure to be built in the UK in the past fifty years. The exceptional complexity and artistic creativity of the precast panels that cloak the Canongate Wall, could only be solved using robotic technology commonly deployed in Formula One racing and the aerospace industry. It has enabled Malling Products to become the market leader in bespoke precast cladding in Europe.

We were involved in the Scottish Parliament buildings through Laing O'Rourke who had won the contract for building the concrete frame. We are a subsidiary company within Laing O'Rourke and were already working on ideas of how to incorporate as many precast elements into the frame as possible because the finished quality had to be very good. We resorted to insitu concrete construction where it was not practical or possible to precast.

We were given one drawing for the Canongate Wall from which to evolve the precast panels and the finishes. The drawing was a combination of a rough sketch, a montage of images that had been cut out of magazines or from photos taken of the surrounding landscape...and some poetry! It frightened the living daylights out of us when we first saw it and were asked to comment on the precasting possibilities. We invited Gary Lucas of Patterns and Moulds to join us at the next construction meeting in the hope that we could find a solution to the problem. His company make a lot of special precast moulds for Malling. We did not want to say yes straightaway and find out later that it was impossible to precast.

We were already working with Patterns and Moulds trying to find an economical way to make latex

moulds for the unique bamboo pattern relief on the flat panels for the MSP boundary walls. The challenge was not how we cast or finished the concrete but how we could make bespoke moulds which were curved along an asymmetric axis and indented with large and small pockets in a random order to receive pieces of natural stone. Using conventional methods of mould making and employing teams of carpenters it would have taken five times longer than the robotic router method that Patterns and Moulds invested in. The cost of the finished concrete using the robotic router was around £1000/m^2. It would have cost at least £6000/m^2 using traditional methods and taken at least three weeks to make each master mould.

CNC (Computer Numeric Controlled) Routers have been used in the aerospace and car manufacturing industry for many years. They are programmed to cut and accurately form three-dimensional shapes. An identical copy of the machine is in the Jordan Formula One factory. There was a specialist company in Loughborough who had a CNC machine and who Patterns and Moulds had hired to cut out the bamboo motifs on MDF board for the special MSP precast walls. So when the sketch for the Canongate wall was further developed by RMJM architects into a CAD model, we knew that

the master mould could be made using upgraded software to drive a CNC machine, which was purchased by Patterns and Moulds for this project.

The 3D model of each panel was generated in AutoCAD by the architects. The CAD image had to be transposed to a CAD/CAM system or MC9file for it to be read by the machine's software. The actual precast panels were 3m by 4.5m in size, but as the machine can only tool or cut mould sizes of not more than 3m by 1.5m we had to split the 3D image into thirds to tool the whole panel. The information in the MC9file tells the CNC machine what cutter diameter is required, the depth and curvature to cut and the line to follow. To program the CNC machine takes a technician about four days sitting in front of a computer.

The critical factor of the system is the quality and accuracy of the AutoCAD drawing that is sent to us. The information input for a CNC machine works to an accuracy of five decimal places, so if adjoining lines on the CAD image are out by less than half a millimetre the machine will not function and results in an error. The software produces the tool path to drive the cutter and sends positioning code signals similar to those of a stereoscopic image of contour lines on an OS map. The cutter has directional information

along the x, y and z axes and the B and C rotational axes. B axis is rotational on plan and C is rotational on elevation. In this way we can programme the machine to cut a perfect sphere if required.

To begin the process a 50mm deep, 3m by 4.5m MDF panel is placed below the router head. The router cuts to a depth of 25mm into the MDF to form the patterns. The router starts by cutting the first 3m by 1.5m section in 14hrs. It can take up to two days to complete the whole panel. The cutting head rotates at 25,000rpm and the cutting tool is changed depending on the stage of the process. The first stage is the rough cut using 16mm to 25mm cutter diameters, when a large amount of material is removed. When the router gets down to the finishing stages, the machine makes hundreds of passes over the panel to bring the cut surface to a smooth finish, using ball-end cutter heads.

The completed MDF panel is waterproofed and varnished and set in a boundary frame. A latex rubber solution which is a two-part thermo-setting polymer resin, is poured over the MDF. It has the consistency of treacle and fills all the depressions and comes to level across the boundary frame. When it has hardened it is lifted out and sent to Malling Products at Grays. The latex rubber mould

is placed in the precast mould frame and a release agent applied. The small stones that appear in the recesses and windows in the panels are then placed in position. Some of the stones were recovered from the old brewery that once occupied the site. Every piece of stone had to be carefully cut to size and shape and placed in the correct recess in the panel before concreting. The very large stones are positioned by crane into the recesses once the panel is in position on site. The Scottish Parliament concrete mix was poured into the mould and left to harden. The mix was a pale grey concrete using ordinary Portland cement and crushed Derbyshire limestone fines.

The 250mm thick precast panel which was reinforced with mesh was left to cure in the mould for 24hours. When the panel was removed some surfaces had to be sand blasted and others left with a lightly polished finish. We had to mask all the fair- face non-blasted surfaces with plastic insulating tape and fill up the stone rebates with weak mortar so that during blasting it would not get eroded, but was easy to remove afterwards. That was the most difficult part of the precasting work at Grays.

An important issue on the Scottish Parliament Building and all precast work is the surface quality

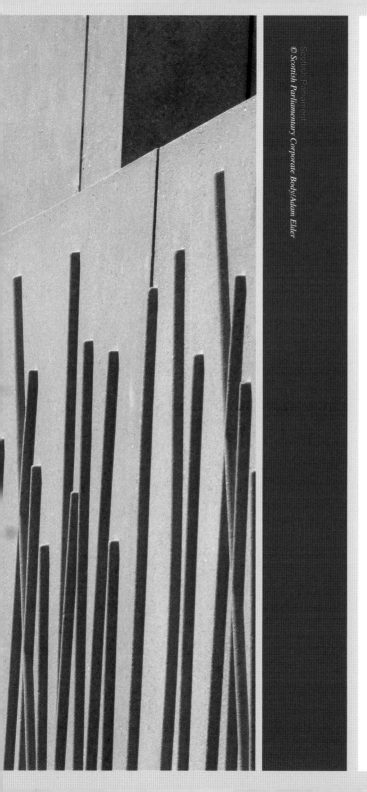

and preciseness of panel construction. Many of the panels had patterns on the surface that were continued onto adjacent units. If we worked to the tolerances we are allowed to use (i.e. + or - 10mm for fixing tolerance, and + or - 6mm for manufacturing tolerances which is collective of + or - 12mm) we could have ugly edges of discontinuity as wide as 15mm to 20mm which are permissible. With the CNC routed moulds we achieved a manufacturing accuracy to within one millimetre of exactness. Although the panels on the Canongate wall were heavy – some of them were 18 tonnes – and there was deflection in the cantilever steel supporting frame as they were positioned, we ended with a positional tolerance of only + or - 2mm which is phenomenal.

When you invest in a CNC machine you have to think about recovery of the capital cost within a five- year period. By that time the machine will be obsolete and you will need to invest in the latest model. The efficiency you gain and the reduction in labour cost you save must be offset against the investment of £140k for the machine and £25k for the software we had to purchase. We can say with confidence it was well worth the savings it made on this project alone, never mind the next five years!

CONCRETE ELEGANCE//
03SPIRAL DREAMS

CRC Challenges Metal for Slimness
The spiral staircase in Tuborg 15 Building, Hellerup

Hans Exner of Ramboll Engineers and Bendt Aarup of CRC Technology

The staircase is located in Tuborg 15 building which is along Tuborg Boulevard in the new urban quarter of Tuborg Havn in Hellerup.

The area was a run down industrial zone only a few years ago, since then it has changed into a vibrant new commercial district of Copenhagen. Tuborg 15 is a purpose built four-storey office building that is leased by three software companies, the focal point of which is the open staircase that spirals down the east elevation of the atrium – a piece of sculptural art. Connected to the floor divisions at landing level only, it is a completely self-supporting structure.

Structural Considerations

Hans Exner, Ramboll Engineers

When we first thought about the spiral staircase we had never heard of CRC (Compact Reinforced Composite) and intended to scheme it in steel or reinforced concrete. It was only by chance when reading a design journal that the architects Arkitema came across CRC. It is a fantastic product. We met with Bendt Aarup from CRC Technology and the spiral staircase evolved.

The architect wished to design the staircase with a double balustrade and no columns and all in white concrete. We persuaded them that it was better structurally to have a column and only an interior balustrade. The column support was necessary as the precast beams at the edge of the building floor were neither robust enough nor thick enough to carry the landing loads from the staircase when we assessed the structure. We could not fix nor tie the balustrade walls to the building floor without having to do some strengthening work to the entire edge of the floor beam. This would have been disruptive, costly and quite unsightly. It should be noted that the staircase was included after the main building had been designed and building floors had been constructed. We also felt that the double balustrade wall would not look as pleasing as it blanks out the transparency and lightness of the staircase.

We proposed a column with an interior balustrade wall acting as a beam from which the steps cantilever out. The leading edge of the steps could be made very thin as there was no force acting on it. The architect accepted our ideas and incorporated that into the final design. However, the column was made as a curved segment of a circle, wider at the base and tapering towards the top and an integral part of the balustrade. It supports the spiral beam and the landing and carries the loads to the foundations. The balustrade beam spans from floor to floor, between the columns. The column restricts the bending and torsion in the balustrade beam. Each staircase step cantilevers as an independent element – we did not allow for any interaction or restraint from the adjacent steps or for the spread of load in our calculations. In reality the steps and risers help each other and ensure an exceptional rigidity of the construction, resulting in zero deflection at the edge under the worst loading conditions. We designed the floor loading as $2.5kN/m^2$ or the equivalent of ten cement bags per square metre across the steps. The landings are connected to the building floor and provide the lateral stability of the staircase structure.

Every element of the spiral staircase is precast with 100Mpa CRC. The flights – which comprise the balustrade beam and cantilever steps – are cast

in four sections and stitched together with insitu JointCast CRC on site. The joints between flights are nominally 80mm wide as the JointCast has an exceptional high bond strength which reduces the joint width. The upper balustrade section connects over the top of the column and links with the landing section. The first flight structure is carefully propped before the upper column element is put in position and the joints then filled.

The design rules for the CRC staircase were taken from standard design rules for reinforced concrete spiral staircases in our codes of practice. The main difference between CRC and conventional concrete, apart from the increase in compressive and tensile strength, is the superior bond strength and anchorage length that we can work to. We can design with very short lengths of starter and lapping bars, only one-fifth of the bond length required for normal concrete. The most critical section was the anchorage length of 100mm required for the rebar of the cantilever steps. Allowing for tolerance and cover, this required the balustrade wall to be 150mm wide. The reinforcement takes all the cantilever bending moment and transfers it to the balustrade beam. Perhaps we could have made the balustrade beam as thin as 100mm and used U bars to develop the anchorage for the steps, but that would have made the joint details with the interconnecting bars of the

balustrade beam too complicated. In any case we felt we needed the 150mm thickness to cater for the bending and torsion in the beam.

When we first proposed a column supporting the balustrade beam we suggested it should be square. The architect came up with the idea of making it 150mm thick, the same as the balustrade, and to curve its width to maintain the curvature of the balustrade. That was a very elegant solution which we then detailed.

In all our design work using CRC we had to justify our calculations and assumptions to the checking authorities. We showed them the long-term test results on durability, bending, anchorage, fatigue, etc. that CRC technology had undertaken over fifteen years. That was sufficient to satisfy them. As regards fire risk, the staircase is not the fire escape stairs for the building and therefore required only a half hour fire rating. The concrete cover to the bars was 15mm (10mm for cover and 5mm tolerance) and we have used 8mm diameter bars in the steps and 16mm bars in the balustrade wall and column.

We did not prepare the staircase prefabrication drawings; we only prepared the reinforcement arrangement drawings and sent them to the architect who pulled all the information together and sent them to the contractor.

CRC (Compact Reinforced Composite) for Precast Applications

Bendt Aarup, CRC Technology

High Strength or High Performance Concretes (HSC or HPC) are used increasingly for a range of structural applications, and standards in a number of countries are being revised to accommodate these improved materials. Often, however, HSC is more brittle than conventional concretes, which can lead to problems in failure mode, as well as under service conditions. One way of overcoming this problem is to provide ductility by incorporating steel fibres in the matrix. Fibre Reinforced Concretes (FRC) have mostly been used in non-structural applications such as slabs-on-grade, floors and architectural concrete and where less than 1% by volume of fibres are used.

CRC is a special type of fibre reinforced high performance concrete developed in 1986 by Aalborg Portland in Denmark which incorporates fibre contents of 2% to 6% by volume corresponding to between 150 and 475kg of steel fibres per m^3 of concrete. In addition to this, the matrix has a very large content of microsilica, plus water/binder ratios of typically 0.2 or lower. This composition makes CRC very dense and well suited for structural applications with a typical mean compressive strength of 150N/mm^2. It is thus possible to utilise

reinforcement much more effectively without having large cracks under service conditions. As CRC is quite different from conventional concrete it has been necessary to provide extensive documentation on the properties of CRC before the material could be considered for structural applications. CRC has been the subject of a number of research projects dealing with structural properties, but also with aspects such as durability and fire resistance.

With the high fibre contents that are somewhat detrimental to workability, CRC is especially suitable for precast applications, but a special type of CRC called CRC JointCast – a mortar with 6% of fibres (475kg/m^3) – is used for insitu cast joints between structural members of ordinary concrete. The Building Research Establishment (BRE) at Watford has investigated this type of application in a project on innovative joints under a DETR Framework Programme. For precast applications a special CRC binder is sold and the production plants are then given advice on casting, which aggregates to use, etc. CRC JointCast is supplied as a dry-mortar – mainly to improve quality control as CRC JointCast is typically used on site. Due to the low water content, CRC has to be protected from evaporation

shortly after casting, and the high content of super plasticizer means that at normal temperatures (20°C) it takes up to 16 hours before elements can be removed from the moulds. Typical strength at one day is 80N/mm^2.

Typical applications for precast work are small and slender elements such as balcony slabs, staircases, small beams and columns. While strength and ductility is much better than for conventional concrete, stiffness is only slightly higher, which means that deformation is one of the aspects that has to be considered carefully in design – especially as CRC is always used in very slender designs. Allowance also has to be made for shrinkage of CRC due to the large binder content. This is usually handled by incorporating additional reinforcement.

The CRC binder is more expensive than cement and the steel fibre content also leads to a higher price for CRC. On the other hand elements are typically one-third the volume of conventional concrete. This means that on the types of applications that have been used in Denmark – typically balcony slabs and staircases – the price for CRC has been equivalent to alternatives in steel or concrete. Obviously in cases where the architect chooses very special solutions this also requires a higher price, but in these cases it has little to do with the price of materials, but more to do with price of formwork and production costs. In a number of cases CRC has been chosen for applications simply because the price was lower than alternatives in steel or concrete. In these cases the engineer or architect has usually chosen a different supporting system for CRC, such as replacing concrete balcony slabs supported on columns with cantilevered CRC slabs.

This challenge of utilising a different type of material in a manner that leads to savings in the total cost has been met by a number of Danish architects. It has lead to several interesting projects just like the spiral staircase at Tuborg 15.

CONCRETE ELEGANCE//
04RESIDENTIAL DELIGHTS

One, Centaur Street, Waterloo
Alex de Rijke, De Rijke Marsh Morgan Architects

Centaur Street was conceived as an 'inside-out' building. Internally the walls are of textured concrete, and externally they are over clad with a chocolate-brown concrete graduated 'timber' rainscreen. The building consists of four apartments, each enjoying a dynamic interior organised as a large, open double-height living space, interpenetrated by adjacent enclosed bedrooms and stairs which form a buffer to the viaduct.

The brief was to create an experimental housing type which examined and exploited the potential of density on small gap sites. The Eurostar viaduct was an unlikely genus loci, but its close proximity generated a clear zoning of the plan; a powerful entry route, with stairs and services, and finally living space, all arranged as parallel strips. The accommodation is varied, intimate and prioritises space and light.

We have been interested in all building materials and the art of construction, working entirely with standardised materials that we find in catalogues. Yet we try to create non-standard architecture by carefully assembling the components. The client, Roger Zogolovitch, came to us with a proposal to design an entirely insitu concrete building, which was quite a challenge as we had never designed with concrete before. It was to be exposed internally and clad externally which is odd because there seems to be a precedent for it to be the other way round in the UK. This project was more about texture and surface quality than composition or colour. It was achieved internally by the process of casting and forming the walls, the floors and the roof. We had a site into which we simply poured concrete right up to the boundaries and

to the rooftops. Had we had more time to reflect and freedom to consider our options we might have elected to go with precast concrete for the staircases. But we had a client who was completely in love with insitu concrete: 'the grey gold' as he would affectionately brand it. He wanted a joint-less, seamless building and I quite understand why. The contractor was not completely equipped or experienced to form it to the standard we had expected, but they made an honest and diligent effort and after the surface was lightly sand blasted we were very satisfied with the resulting cave-like quality. There is something wonderful about this material; it is the structure and architecture, it is not stitched together, bolted or nailed. We can design double-height load bearing walls, overhanging cantilever slabs and neo-georgian steps in concrete.

Our working relations with the client who was an architect, was both open and exacting and a strange intense process. It was the paradox of having an architect commission you to design his own building, but he trusted us enough to let us bring our ideas forward and infuse them into the design. We had board marking on some walls; making it in softwood and flat finish in the bedrooms using phenolic resin overlaid plywood panels. We enjoyed the illusion of wood that the internal concrete conveys. On the outside we had fibre-cement board marked panels, pretending to be wood very effectively and maintenance free. It was an Eternit product that was developed for weather boarding on seaside chalets but not on a building. Since we have adapted it as a rainscreen on our building, we have seen it copied everywhere.

This building is didactic, the cladding does not cover up the weather-tight insulation behind it, and the insulation does not hide the load-bearing structure nor does the structure hide the finished architecture. It's a layered composite design like the vest, shirt and jacket of clothing that you can see at the edges. I think building architecture goes down hill once the main structure is covered up like the upholstery of a furniture frame. I hate the notion that you need five trades to make a wall – stud frame, plaster board, insulation, plaster and paint. Concrete is the perfect medium for house construction – it has character, it can support itself, it is self-finished and is one process.

We introduced recycled materials from the construction in the furniture and flooring of our new office in the ground floor apartment. The plywood

which had a phenolic resin overlay and which was used for the floor slabs, was also used for the bookshelves. We used new panels of the rough boarded timber laths that formed the board-marked wall to make into a sliding door. We tried to limit the palette of materials by using the formwork that cast the concrete. The glass parquet on the ground floor was recycled from the glass that was supplied incorrectly for the louvers on the stairwell and the window box on the east elevation. I could not bear to see such beautiful glass thrown into a skip. We retrieved them and had the sheets cut into 300mm squares with bevelled edges. However, to lay the glass parquet on a fire-retarded, styrofoam substrate has proved a technical nightmare. A self-levelling screed was poured over the existing floor which was not flat enough for the styrofoam. The styrofoam has routed ducts for running the computer cables and for sleeving the under floor heating pipes and, once these were in position, we placed an acrylic sheet over the support ridges to distribute the load and to bed the parquet to the foam substrate. The glass panels are held down by double sided adhesive tape and the joint edges sealed with glass glue. We found the glue was too brittle and de-bonded with the slightest movement, so we replaced it with silicone and that seems to work well.

The spatial organisation of the interior is based on the Raumplan principle pioneered by Adolf Loos. The double-height central space has a tight mezzanine floor slotted into it with smaller self-contained rooms leading off to the sides. This was not to be a static event with rooms assembled in rows around a central staircase, like a terraced Victorian house. Here the smaller rooms wrap around the large void and are interconnected by a series of discrete stairs. It is a hybrid of the open plan European apartment and the English vertical terraced house and it works well.

Aberdeen Lane, Islington
Ferhan Azman, Azman Architects

This new build house for a family of six is located on an unadopted lane dominated by workshops, studios and light industrial sheds.

The site backs on to an established residential neighbourhood. This trend-setting modern house in Islington is a statement in wall-to-wall insitu concrete. What is so surprising about the concrete is its marble-smooth finish, its flawlessly clean surface and seamless appearance.

The focus of the brief was to create a house with sufficient space and comfort for a family of six. The site is bordered by a detached house on the west side, terraced mews houses on the east side and a garden wall at the rear. The starting point of the concept was the decision on the orientation of the house. The decision to face the house inwards to create a courtyard rather than face the lane was followed by a series of decisions that led to the choice of materials and method of construction. It was decided that the north and south walls to the house (the walls facing the lane and the house at the rear) would be treated as solid without many openings, in order to maintain a definitive edge to the lane and avoid overlooking. The other instrumental parameter was the depth of the mews house at the east side of the site. With these two critical considerations the house was designed as two interlocking cubes of internally and externally exposed reinforced concrete walls. The choice of concrete was driven by the desired solidness of the north and south walls. We wanted these walls to be seamless planes and proposed concrete to the client. The house was designed like a doll's house with a west facing 'courtyard' façade left transparent with large panes of glass in timber framing. This responds to the client's brief for the

house to accommodate the varying needs of a large family. Timber louvers are installed at first floor level for a degree of privacy.

We chose to use the same materials throughout the house internally and externally, which are limited to concrete, limestone, timber and glass, apart from the quaint guest bathroom built in stainless steel with a red rubber floor.

Aberdeen Lane in Islington is a bit off the beaten track, along a dirt road, past a collection of single storey warehouses, back gardens and drab garages. Why build something so ultra modern and spanking new down a long uninviting industrial lane, in the shadow of a 1920s brick built mansion. For the client this site was perfect – it's a five minute walk from the tube station and a ten minute car ride into the city; it's in a very sought after location, but more to the point it was a plot of land within their budget. The client thought the site interesting and private. The location gave us the opportunity to create something dramatic and monolithic in appearance – there were no buildings close by to relate to. Instinctively our thoughts went to insitu concrete and when we suggested it to the client they were surprised but not shocked. What was causing the greatest anxiety to both architect

and client was finding a contractor who would price the job within budget and also execute the concrete beautifully; a notion that many designers think are mutually incompatible objectives. Varbud Construction in Perivale had worked for the architects before on refurbishment projects – they made furniture, fitted out retail units, built handmade kitchens, did all the plastering, plumbing and brickwork; even cast concrete floors and walls and were always very competitive on their pricing. They were keen to take on Aberdeen Lane and we trusted their integrity knowing how carefully they work, but fair-face insitu concrete was going to be a new challenge for them. This bold project was going to establish their reputation.

The double skin concrete walls of the box structure act as bookends, retaining the open glass elevations that look westwards over the courtyard garden, the large ash tree, the iroko panelled timber garage and garden room. The concrete inner walls support the concrete first floor slab, the flat roof and the staircase. The living spaces are all on the ground floor – the kitchen, lounge, TV room and dining area, with the bedrooms on the first floor. They are accessed via an open plan precast staircase that runs along the double-height east wall, whose roof light floods the staircase in

daylight. Single skin block work walls divide the internal spaces of the house into its functional uses – bedrooms, bathrooms, walk-in wardrobes and so on. All the 200mm thick inner load-bearing concrete walls and the floors were cast before the 150mm outer skin of the concrete cavity walls was constructed. The finished concrete surface is marble-smooth to touch, light grey in colour and full of subtle abstract flecks and variations depending on the angle of the light. How was it achieved? After the contractor had completed the sample panels to check the efficiency of different release agents, they machine cut the large birch-faced ply sheets in their workshops and prepared the surface by sanding it down, then coating it with two coats of lacquer.

Once on site the birch-faced panels were lightly oiled with a high performance chemical release agent manufactured by Nufins, before they were screw fixed to the backing ply. They were not allowed to screw fix on the fair-face side of the ply. Everything had to be screwed from the back of the panels. In addition, the strongbacks and walings to support the forms were designed with no tie-bolts over the body of the formwork. A–Plant, who supplied all the props, had never designed temporary works with quite this degree

of sophistication and control, but it worked very well. The push–pull props in the mid-span, the close centred walings over the lower half and the double row of strongbacks, kept the shutters rigid and true under the 3m head of liquid concrete. The concrete walls are as straight as a pole, perfectly plumb, with no lipping or bowing over their height. Wacker UK Ltd arranged a training workshop to show the concrete ganger how to use their constant amplitude pokers effectively. We were supplied with the best concrete we have ever seen for consistency of mix and workability by Hanson Premix. Their service to the site has been first class.

We wanted a smooth-faced, light grey concrete that would not become dirt-encrusted or stained. What has been achieved has come up to all our expectations. The surface is sensual, cool and very tactile and makes a strong contrast with the limestone ground floor tiles, the wooden framed windows, and the elm covered first floor panels.

CONCRETE ELEGANCE//
05SCULPTURAL
INSPIRATIONS

Concrete as Art
Carole Vincent, Artist

Carole Vincent is Britain's foremost artist working in concrete. She is a painter and sculptor by training who lives in Boscastle, Cornwall.

Her large-scale commissions have included the award winning sundial and fountain in Plymouth town square, 'The Pedestrians' in Devon, 'Quartet' in Glasgow and 'Colloquy Two' in Singapore to name but a few. The 'Bude Light' in Cornwall and The Blue Circle Garden at the Chelsea Flower Show, both of which received Certificates of Excellence from the Concrete Society, are her more recent major works.

Boscastle with its harbour and surrounding cliff landscape has been a major influence on my work in sculpture and in painting for over forty years. I live at the top of the village in an old stone cottage with roses round the front door. It has a gallery upstairs, a converted piggery as one studio and a purpose built studio for working in concrete and then I have an acre of garden, developed from a field and divided into three distinct areas of cottage garden, a wild wood and concrete garden.

Concrete has always been a significant part of my life. My father's building firm had a small concrete works and I remember making concrete blocks as a child. I only began to realise concrete's sculptural potential in 1982 when I was asked to make the sculpture 'Reunion' for my former headmistress. It was too large for carving in stone and too bulky for casting in bronze. A chance meeting with a professional plaster mould maker showed me how I could work in clay, make a plaster mould and then fill it with concrete. It was not very good concrete at first because I used recipes provided by artists and not those in the precast industry. When I designed the piece 'One and All' I sought advice from the precast company Minsterstone who were very generous in providing materials and recipes. More small works followed and the concrete finish

became better polished with different aggregates making changes of colour. The Armada Dial in 1988 which comprises a sundial and fountain in Plymouth City Centre gave me the break that every artist dreams of. A major work on a scale that was not possible to cast in the studio.
I produced the maquettes, drafted the sundial specification and the fountain design and a contractor built it.

Several commissions followed – the *Pedestrians*, *Quartet*, *Colloquy* and *Les Jonglers* in Jersey. My concrete vocabulary changed from the approximations of a builder's yard to the precision and controlled output of a scientific laboratory. I became obsessed with particle size, the grading of aggregates, natural colours and the water–cement ratio of the concrete. Surface grinding, polishing and lacquering techniques were perfected. Before 1992, all my work was with natural aggregates, stone looka-likes, but in the summer of '92 I had a chance to experiment with colour and pigments. I knew that earth-coloured pigments existed, the red and yellow oxides plus back and cyanine blue. If I could have blue I thought, why not a spectrum of red, yellow, green and purple? It's been used in pottery for centuries. Again, a serendipitous meeting led me to source true primary pigments

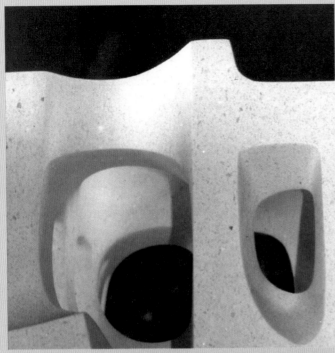

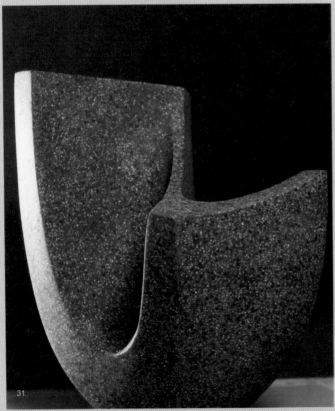

for colouring concrete. Many, many experiments allowed me to sort out those pigments that were compatible with concrete. Architects, engineers, contractors and precast manufacturers were sceptical with my approach. They argued that pigmented colour in concrete fades, the colours are unstable and who wants colour anyway? I did! I wanted to cast pictures with coloured concrete mortars. A still life, a pot and a bowl, a sundial and other pieces followed. They were different, they were multi-coloured, they did not fade and I had created my new concrete art form. The Jonathan Ball practice worked with me and Anthony Fanshawe to produce the *Bude Light* sculpture in 2000, a tribute to the inventor of the *Bude Light*, Sir Goldsworthy Gurney, and a clear statement of what you can do with pigmented colour in concrete.

It was becoming apparent to me that sculpture and the environment were synonymous, as Sir Frederic Gibberd had concluded many years ago when he designed his wonderful garden in Harlow. My garden has also proved it is possible to combine hardscape and sculpture with plants. In the summer of 2000, Elwen Balfour of the Brunswick Group was sitting in my garden and said, "This garden must go to Chelsea – I'll see what I can do." Blue Circle Cement agreed to be the sponsors of a show garden at Chelsea – it was called the Blue Circle Garden and earned a bronze medal from the RHS. The large sphere in the garden has fibre optical lighting. Before casting the piece, dozens of fibres were threaded through the fibreglass mould, bunched together into a cable that comes out of the base and leads to the projector. The problem was filling the mould with a cat's cradle of fibres inside.

In January 2001, I was talking to Ian Hart of Pieri, now part of Grace Products and he told me what I really wanted was a concrete mix that I could pour like plaster into a mould that did not require compaction. He said, "Have you heard of self-compacting concrete; SCC for short?". It's produced with carefully selected and blended fine aggregates and cement, plus superplasticisers and a viscosity agent. It makes free flowing concrete with low water–cement ratios that do not need vibration or compaction. It carries the aggregates to all surfaces and produces a hard, compact surface virtually devoid of air bubbles and voids. It sounded wonderful! No more ramming and the potential to cast intricate shapes with holes.

As a sculptor I work on very small-scale projects. All my experiments with concrete were done in a Kenwood Mixer with 1500g of concrete. A conventional concrete slump test would not work, so I converted to using yoghurt pots and made mixes that achieved a 175mm flow on the table when they were poured out of the pot. It worked. I soon discovered that certain aggregates were better than others; that every pigment has a different workability and required different plasticiser dosages. The stiff mixes that I had used previously were not as sensitive, but they had to be rammed and compacted in the mould in layers and this produced bands of colour. The flowing SCC mixes produce fluid patches of colour that are so different and exciting, like patches of paint on the surface yet they retain their crisp colour edge. Without SCC I would not have been able to fill the mould of my latest sculpture 'Houmet Florains'. This building-like sculpture is based on an abstraction of the ruin of a Victorian Fort at Alderney built in 1850. I made one in white and one in black and hope to use it for a memorial in Jersey for Pat Carter who founded the Jersey Public Sculpture Trust.

Concrete as Art
David Undery, Artist

After graduating from Southampton Institute with a Fine Arts Degree in 1997, David Undery wasted no time in developing his 'concrete' fine art career with exhibitions in a number of art galleries across the UK.

He describes his work as abstract paintings in concrete even though some of the work is highly sculptural. His work crosses the boundaries between painting and sculpture to create wall hangings that combine lustrous colours with satin-soft or highly polished surfaces. Through his own dedicated passion for concrete, he transforms the material into a truly unique, aesthetic art form.

I started off as a figurative painter at art school working in oils and painting portraits. After a year I began an interest in painting cityscapes, inspired by the building and architecture of Southampton and the concrete pavement slabs that I walked on every day. Many of the buildings were precast, particularly near the railway station, and were very dominating structures. The weather patterning and texture on the concrete surfaces was intriguing, particularly the markings on pavement slabs absorbed from rainwater run-off, spillage of drinks, the resin stains from leaves and other detritus. The cityscapes I was painting were based on concrete colours and I thought it would be fun to add some neat cement in with the oils when I painted on the canvas. I started by sprinkling cement dust on the oils over the hardscape areas which became more intense towards the base of the canvas. The cement caused the surface to become lumpy and flake away. I then thought of washing the canvas with cement slurry over the bottom third to create the hardscape colour then continue with oils above that. I added a poly-vinyl-acrylic (PVA) to the water as a bonding agent to help the cement adhere to the canvas. Some parts of the picture would be oil paints and others neat cement and I found that the bigger the painting the better the cement

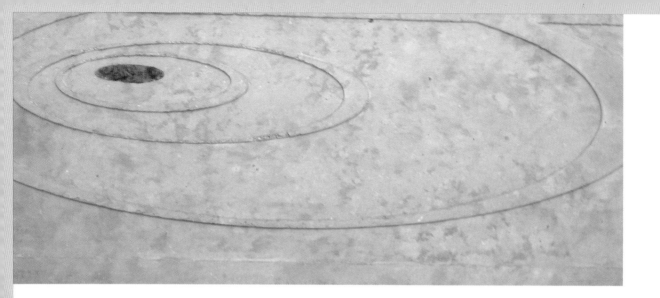

slurry worked with the oil as a composition. When I attempted to lift the canvas, bits of cement mortar would crack and fall out because the canvas was so flexible. So I started using hardboard to lay the cement mortar on and worked on 12ft wide by 6ft high compositions consisting of nine separate panels 4ft by 2ft. The bottom three panels were made of cement mortar cast on hardboard into which I had inserted pipe work and bits of glass like an abstraction of building materials. The panels become very heavy; some were more than 50mm thick. They were paving slabs with a hardboard backing! It was by chance when I had taken down the upper panels from the wall of the art room and had just the three concrete ones left on view, that I realised what I liked most about the composition – it was the concrete panels. So from that day on I started to concentrate on painting with concrete panels.

The technology of concrete mixing and making durable concrete was new to me. I found out the hard way that you must not add too much water to the mix, that you can't use poster colours for pigments, that reinforcement is required for tensile strength to reduce the thickness of the panel and to ensure it will not break when lifted. I had learnt about water/cement ratios by the time I had

finished my degree but had not discovered the world of concrete pigments and colour. The college tutors did not have much knowledge of concrete and what I knew was self-taught. I had only been experimenting using grey monochrome concrete, tooling and etching the surface by the time I left art school.

I discovered concrete pigments when I went to a builders' merchant to buy cement and also noted that you can get white and grey cement. Walking past construction sites I observed they were using reinforcing bars to strengthen concrete slabs, not the small bore metal pipes that I had been trying. Next I did some research on concrete mixes and pigments, surface texturing and profiling using reference books and publications on architectural concrete that I found in the library. I found out about chemical stains and dry shake pigments from suppliers Hatfields in Yorkshire. When I approached a gallery in Southampton who were keen to display my art, they were genuinely concerned about the durability of the panel; whether it would last more than a year if it was made with concrete. I reassured them that it would outlast the life of the buyer.

With my concrete canvas the whole surface was

differentially pigmented and varied in texture and surface appearance, unlike traditional precast panels or paving slabs which have the same unifying surface colour or texture throughout. Combinations of natural materials like wood and stone even copper are inserted into the concrete canvas whose colour is as rippled and layered as a veneer of beautiful rosewood or cherry wood. The lustre of the surface finishes are brought about by coating the hardened concrete with special clear lacquers. This intensifies the base colour pigments and heightens the minute particles of sand grains and micro-pores that appear on the surface as though carried on a lava-like flow. It reminds me of a star cluster or a nebula gas cloud in the Milky Way. The lava or toffee effect of colour on the surface is created by tilting the panel slightly when the cement has just set and pouring a small amount of acid etch on one corner and watching it mingle, disturb and dissolve the surface colour slowly into a paste that trickles down the face. I sometimes introduce copper as this patinates with the acid etch to release a turquoise green into the colour flow.

When the concrete has fully hardened I apply different textures by further acid etching or adding chemical stains which react with the free lime to dye the substrate terracotta, black or green. Many of my compositions have elliptical motifs and colour bands that add emphasis to the shape and textures that I have created. I have recently started to experiment with polishing and abrading the surface with discs to express the aggregates, cutting into the panel, forming drifts and strata of colour moving away from surface colouring and highly glazed pieces. This is my new concrete stone effect paintings that may lead me on to sculptural art one day. There seems no end to concrete's versatility, plasticity and creative possibilities.

CONCRETE ELEGANCE//
06 PREFABRICATED PERFECTION

The Seonyu Footbridge, Seoul
A New Ultra High Performance Concrete DUCTAL©
Mouloud Behloul, Lafarge, France

The Seonyu footbridge links the main town of Seoul to Sunyudo Island across the Han river.

The footbridge, which was built in time for the World Cup in 2000 was called 'The Bridge of Peace' when it was opened but has since reverted to its official name. It consists of two steel approach spans and a central arch of 120m made of Ductal, a new ultra high performance concrete. Before describing how we were able to precast the bridge segments and build this very slender concrete arch, let me first explain what Ductal is and how the material differs from conventional concrete.

Ductal is a concrete composed of cement particles, fibres, special fillers and plasticisers that is able to fully hydrate with the minimum of added water. It has a water/cement ratio of just 0.20. It belongs to a special group of ultra high performance fibre reinforced concretes, referred to as UHPFRC. Ductal is the outcome of over ten years of collaborative research between Lafarge the material manufacturer, Bouygues the contractor and Rhodia, a chemical manufacturer. Through intensive research and development work, the material has been patented, refined and commercialised. Fifteen universities and six testing laboratories in different countries have also contributed to the research effort.

In May 2002, design guidance rules and material recommendations were formulated in France for the use of Ductal in structural applications. These recommendations were established by a working group comprised of representatives from leading construction companies, building control agencies, suppliers, certification authorities and coordinated by SETRA (Road and Traffic Government Agency).

The material consists of cement and cementitious fillers carefully blended and graded, with a particle size distribution ranging from a maximum of 600µm (0.6mm) down to less than 0.1µm to obtain the densest packing with the minimum of void spaces. It has no sand fines or coarse aggregates. It is a super high strength concrete mortar with the minimum of internal and external imperfections such as micro-cracks, air voids and pore spaces. This enables the material to achieve a greater percentage of its ultimate load-carrying capacity and enhances its durability properties.

The material has a compressive strength ranging from 200Mpa to 350Mpa, but does not have sufficient ductility. The inclusion of steel fibres drastically improves the tensile strength and provides a substantial level of ductility. The various formulations and applications of Ductal that we have commercialised are based on an optimisation of the material composition with steel and organic fibres. For example, to enhance its structural performance steel fibres are included and the material is also heat treated to reduce creep and shrinkage strain. For every application the technology can be adjusted to achieve the optimum performance required.

For structural grades, Ductal®-FM is prescribed, for a smooth decorative material that can be handled Ductal®-FO which has organic fibres is prescribed, and for enhanced fire resistance Ductal®-AF is prescribed which has a combination of steel and organic (polypropylene) fibres.

The fresh mixing of these materials with the controls that we have introduced makes it relatively easy to handle in terms of flow and self-compaction. With minor adjustments, most conventional concrete batching equipment is suitable for mixing Ductal. The Ductal matrix gives a very fine 'bone china' surface finish that can be moulded to replicate any kind of profile or intricate pattern. By using adequate pigments a range of coloured concretes can be achieved for architectural and decorative applications.

Ductal®-FM, with a compressive strength of 180Mpa, was specified for the Seonyu bridge where high bending and direct tensile strengths are required. These mechanical properties are achieved by introducing short steel fibres 13–15mm in length with a diameter of 0.2mm at a dosage of 2% of the mix volume. The application of heat treatment after the mix sets in the mould eliminates drying shrinkage and greatly reduces creep.

Table 1. Properties (typical values) of Ductal® with steel fibres and after heat treatment.

Density	2500 kg/m^3
Compressive strength	180 MPa
Tensile strength	8 MPa
Post-peak strength in tension	5 MPa
Young's modulus	50 000 MPa
Poisson's ratio	0.2
Shrinkage	0
Creep factor	0.2
Thermal expansion coefficient	12.10^{-6} m/m

Table 2. Load-deflection under three-point loading

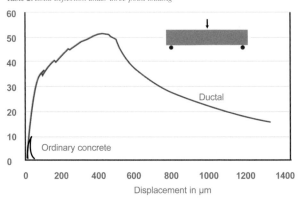

A typical load–deflection curve for Ductal under a three-point loading test is shown in table 2. The material exhibits linear elastic behaviour up to first crack and has considerable ductility thereafter until the ultimate flexure load is reached, whereupon it begins to yield with plastic failure until rupture. It has an ultimate bending strength which is over twice its first crack stress and more than ten times the ultimate stress of conventional mortars. With such high strength and ductility, Ductal allows us to design structures without any secondary passive reinforcement and no shear reinforcement.

The main properties of the Ductal that was cast in the bridge sections in Seoul, are given in table 1.

The Ductal Arch

The 120m arch is connected at each end to massive reinforced concrete foundations which are 9m deep. These foundations are designed to absorb the horizontal thrust of the arch. The arch consists of a ribbed upper deck slab (the walkway) and two girder beams in a double T configuration. The width of the deck slab is 4.3m and the beams are 1.3m deep. The deck slab has a 30mm topping with transverse ribs at 600mm centres that are 150mm deep. The deck slab is supported by the two 160mm thick girder beams. The shape of the girder beams and deck slab geometry was chosen for easy demoulding of the section.

The ribs of the deck slab are prestressed by either one or two 12.5mm diameter monostrands. Specially adapted small anchors were used to transfer the prestressing forces from the strands to the ribs. Each girder beam is prestressed longitudinally by three tendon clusters which are sleeved through metal ducts. There are nine strands in each of the clusters in the lower two ducts and twelve strands in the upper duct. The tendons of the beams are stressed once the segments are in place on the supporting scaffold towers. After completion of the stressing phase, the tendon ducts are grouted. Two temporary monostrands are cast into each segment in the lower part of the beam to cater for stresses during lifting and placing operations as each segment is positioned onto the scaffold towers that were built across the river.

The arch is composed of six segments. These segments are prefabricated in an area next to the final location of the arch. Diaphragms are added at the ends of each segment. The diaphragms on the end of the segments spread the compressive loads impacting on the foundation concrete, while those

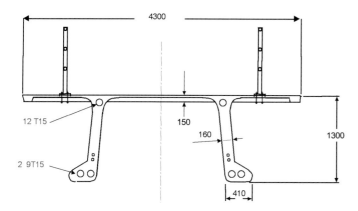

over the central arch are for jacking the two halves of the arch.

The segments are 20–22m long and curved. The slope at the extremities is more than 8%. The volume of Ductal in a segment is 22.5m^3. The total mixing time to fill the metal mould for each segment was five and a half hours. The mould is filled using eight injection points positioned midway along the internal surface of the beams. During the casting operations, the fluidity of the Ductal mix is constantly checked and controlled.

After casting a segment, it is cured in the mould at 35°C for 48 hours. A spreader beam is used to crane lift the segment from the casting area to a heat treatment chamber. The segment is then steam cured at 90°C for 48 hours.

The six segments – three on each half of the arch – are positioned in sequence on the scaffold towers by a crane, mounted on a river barge. The segments on each of the half spans are stitched together, then prestressed before the tendon ducts are grouted. The two half spans are finally joined together by casting the short insitu crown or key segment stitch. Before casting the insitu stitch a precompression force of 2300kN is applied to each half span using hydraulic jacks. The key segment stitch is then cast and when the Ductal in the stitch has reached a strength of 85MPa, the jack loads are removed and the force transfers back into the arch, to maintain the arch in precompression. This is good for stability and robustness.

This is the first time in the world that an ultra high performance concrete, reinforced with steel fibres, has been used for a span of 120m. The properties of Ductal have made it possible to design a very slender arch with thin sections, giving the footbridge elegance. Other footbridges have been constructed using Ductal: they are the Sakata Mirai in Japan, the Sermaises in France, the Sherbrooke in Canada and another one is under construction in Japan.

The use of this concrete-like material has almost unlimited possibilities of appearance, texture and colour. It has excited architects by giving them access to an unexpected new world of shapes and forms. Ductal has been used in architectural applications like bus shelters in Tucson (USA), flower pots in Rennes (France), façade panels in Monaco and the Kyoto clock tower in Japan.

The Concrete Centre

Riverside House
4 Meadows Business Park
Station Approach, Blackwater
Camberley, Surrey GU17 9AB

t: 01276 606800

www.concretecentre.com

For free help and advice on the design,
use and performance of concrete, please call
The Concrete Centre's national helpline
on 0700 4 500 500 or 0700 4 CONCRETE

All Concrete Elegance events are free of charge
and take place in the Building Centre in the
evenings. To attend any event or to find out about
current and future programmes please contact
The Concrete Centre or the Building Centre Trust.